MW01227657

Contents

Introduction to Artificial Intelligence

Artificial Intelligence (AI) is no longer a distant dream or a futuristic concept confined to the realms of science fiction. Today, AI is an integral part of our daily lives, influencing how we work, communicate, learn, and play. AI is everywhere, from the virtual assistants on our smartphones to the recommendation engines guiding our entertainment choices. But what exactly is AI, and how did it evolve to become such a pivotal technology?

At its core, AI is the simulation of human intelligence processes by machines, particularly computer systems. These processes include learning (acquiring information and rules for using the information), reasoning (using rules to reach approximate or definite conclusions), and self-correction. AI encompasses various technologies and approaches, such as machine learning, deep learning, natural language processing, and robotics, each contributing to the broader goal of creating systems that can perform tasks that typically require human intelligence.

The journey of AI began in the mid-20th century, marked by the pioneering work of researchers like Alan Turing and

John McCarthy. Turing's question, "Can machines think?" and his subsequent development of the Turing Test laid the groundwork for future AI research. McCarthy, often referred to as the father of AI, coined the term "artificial intelligence" in 1956 during the famous Dartmouth Conference, which is considered the birth of AI as a field of study.

Over the decades, AI has experienced several waves of optimism, known as AI summers, and periods of skepticism, known as AI winters. Early successes in symbolic AI, which involved high-level human-like reasoning, were followed by challenges in scalability and adaptability. The advent of machine learning, where systems learn from data rather than explicit programming, marked a significant shift, leading to breakthroughs in speech recognition, image analysis, and game-playing.

Today, we stand at the threshold of a new era in AI, driven by unprecedented computational power, vast amounts of data, and innovative algorithms. Deep learning, a subset of machine learning, has enabled AI systems to achieve superhuman performance in various tasks, from defeating world champions in games like Go to diagnosing diseases with greater accuracy than human doctors.

The applications of AI are vast and varied, spanning industries such as healthcare, transportation, finance, education, and entertainment. In healthcare, AI is revolutionizing diagnostics, personalized medicine, and patient care. Autonomous vehicles are set to transform transportation, promising safer and more efficient travel. Financial institutions leverage AI for fraud detection, risk management, and personalized financial services. In education, AI-driven tools are personalizing learning experiences and improving educational outcomes.

However, the rise of AI also brings significant challenges and ethical considerations. As AI systems become more integrated into our lives, issues of privacy, security, bias, and accountability become increasingly critical. Ensuring that AI is developed and deployed responsibly is paramount to harnessing its potential for the greater good.

This book explores the multifaceted world of AI, examining its current state, future prospects, and the profound impact it will likely have on society. Through a comprehensive exploration of advancements in AI technologies, applications across various domains, and the ethical and societal implications, we will gain a deeper understanding of AI's future.

As we embark on this journey, it is essential to recognize that the future of AI is not predetermined. It will be shaped by the choices we make today as researchers, policymakers, industry leaders, and global citizens. By fostering a collaborative and ethical approach to AI development, we can ensure that this transformative technology benefits all of humanity, creating an intelligent, inclusive, and inspiring future.

CHAPTER 1

What is Artificial Intelligence?

Artificial Intelligence (AI) is a term that is becoming increasingly common in everyday language, yet its precise meaning can often be elusive. A clear definition and an exploration of AI's core are essential for understanding its potential and implications.

1.1 Defining Artificial Intelligence

At its most basic level, AI refers to the development of computer systems that can perform tasks typically requiring human intelligence. These tasks include learning from experience, understanding natural language, recognizing patterns, solving problems, and making decisions. AI can be divided into two broad categories: narrow AI and general AI.

Narrow AI, also known as weak AI, is designed and trained for a specific task, such as voice recognition or image classification. These systems are highly specialized and operate under a limited set of parameters. Examples of narrow AI include virtual assistants like Siri and Alexa, recommendation algorithms used by Netflix and Amazon, and the facial recognition systems employed by social media platforms and security agencies.

General AI, or strong AI, refers to systems with generalized human cognitive abilities. When faced with an unfamiliar task, a robust AI system can find a solution without human intervention. While this level of AI remains theoretical and is a subject of ongoing research, achieving general AI would signify a monumental technological leap.

1.2 Historical Context

The concept of artificial intelligence is not new. Philosophers and scientists have long pondered the nature of human thought and whether it could be replicated by machines. However, the formal study of AI began in the mid-20th century.

A British mathematician, Alan Turing, is often credited with laying the groundwork for AI. In his 1950 paper, "Computing Machinery and Intelligence," Turing proposed what is now known as the Turing Test. This test evaluates a machine's ability to exhibit intelligent behavior indistinguishable from a human's. If a human evaluator cannot reliably tell the machine from a human based on their responses, the machine is considered to have passed the test.

The term "artificial intelligence" was coined in 1956 by **John McCarthy** during the Dartmouth Conference, which is considered the founding event of AI as a field. The conference brought together researchers who would become leaders in

AI, including Marvin Minsky, Nathaniel Rochester, and Claude Shannon.

1.3 Core Concepts and Techniques

Exploring some of the key concepts and techniques that underpin AI is helpful in understanding how it works.

Machine Learning (ML) is a subset of AI that involves the development of algorithms that allow computers to learn from and make predictions based on data. Instead of being explicitly programmed to perform a task, machine learning systems use statistical techniques to identify patterns in data and improve their performance over time. There are several types of machine learning, including supervised learning, unsupervised learning, and reinforcement learning.

Supervised Learning involves training a model on a labeled dataset, where the correct output is known. The model makes predictions and is corrected when it makes errors, allowing it to learn over time. Typical applications include spam detection, image recognition, and language translation.

Unsupervised Learning deals with unlabeled data, which aims to identify hidden patterns or intrinsic structures in the input data. Clustering algorithms, which group similar data points together, are a typical example of unsupervised learning techniques.

Reinforcement Learning is a type of machine learning in which an agent learns to make decisions by taking actions in an environment to maximize some notion of cumulative reward. This approach is used in various applications, from gameplay to robotic control.

Deep Learning, a subset of machine learning, involves neural networks with many layers (hence "deep") that can model complex patterns in large amounts of data. Deep learning has been instrumental in achieving breakthroughs in areas such as speech recognition, image processing, and natural language processing.

Natural Language Processing (NLP) is another crucial area of AI that focuses on the interaction between computers and humans through language. NLP enables machines to understand, interpret, and generate human language. Applications of NLP include chatbots, sentiment analysis, and language translation.

1.4 AI in Practice

AI is already making significant impacts across various sectors. In healthcare, AI algorithms assist in diagnosing diseases, personalizing treatment plans, and predicting patient outcomes. For instance, AI-powered imaging systems can detect abnormalities in medical scans with remarkable accuracy, sometimes surpassing human radiologists.

In the automotive industry, AI is the driving force behind autonomous vehicles. These vehicles rely on complex AI systems to process data from sensors, navigate environments, and make real-time decisions to ensure passenger safety.

Financial services use AI for fraud detection, risk assessment, and automated trading. AI models analyze transaction patterns to identify fraudulent activities and help financial institutions mitigate risks.

Retail businesses leverage AI for personalized marketing, inventory management, and customer service. Recommendation engines analyze customer preferences to suggest products, while chatbots provide instant support and assistance.

1.5 The Road Ahead

AI's journey is one of continuous evolution and discovery. As we move forward, its potential applications are boundless. AI promises a transformative future, from enhancing productivity and efficiency to solving some of the world's most pressing challenges.

However, this future also comes with responsibilities. As AI systems become more advanced and pervasive, addressing ethical considerations, ensuring fairness and transparency, and mitigating potential risks is essential. The development of AI must be guided by principles prioritizing human well-being and societal benefit.

In the following chapters, we will delve deeper into specific advancements in AI, explore its applications across various domains, and examine the ethical and societal implications. By understanding the full spectrum of AI's capabilities and challenges, we can better prepare for and shape the future of this remarkable technology.

CHAPTER 2

Advancements in Machine Learning and Deep Learning

Machine Learning (ML) and Deep Learning (DL) are at the heart of the recent AI revolution. These technologies have enabled unprecedented progress in fields as diverse as healthcare, finance, transportation, and entertainment. This chapter will explore the key advancements in ML and DL, their applications, and the future directions these technologies will likely take.

2.1 Basics of Machine Learning

Machine Learning is a subset of AI that focuses on building systems that learn from data and improve over time without being explicitly programmed. The key idea is that exposing an algorithm to large amounts of data can identify patterns and make decisions based on this data.

There are three main types of machine learning:

- **Supervised Learning**: The algorithm is trained on a labeled dataset, meaning each training example is paired with an output label. The model learns to map inputs to outputs and is tested on new, unseen data. Common algorithms include linear regression, decision trees, and support vector machines.

- **Unsupervised Learning**: The algorithm is given data without explicit instructions on what to do with it. Instead, it tries to find hidden patterns or intrinsic structures within the data. Clustering and dimensionality reduction are typical unsupervised learning techniques. K-means and hierarchical clustering are popular algorithms in this category.

- **Reinforcement Learning**: The algorithm learns by interacting with an environment and receiving feedback through rewards or penalties. This type of learning is particularly effective in scenarios where the sequence of actions is crucial, such as in game playing or robotic control. Key concepts include the agent, environment, actions, states, and rewards. Algorithms like Q-learning and deep Q-networks (DQNs) are widely used in reinforcement learning.

2.2 Deep Learning: An Evolution of Machine Learning

Deep Learning, a subset of machine learning, utilizes neural networks with many layers (hence "deep") to analyze various data. These deep neural networks can model complex patterns and representations, making them highly effective for tasks like image and speech recognition.

Key components of deep learning include:

- **Artificial Neural Networks (ANNs)**: Inspired by the human brain, ANNs consist of layers of nodes (neurons) that process data and learn to make decisions. Each connection between nodes has a weight that is adjusted during training to minimize error.

- **Convolutional Neural Networks (CNNs)**: Primarily used for image processing, CNNs apply convolutional layers to scan through images and detect patterns such as edges, textures, and shapes, making them highly effective for tasks like object detection and facial recognition.

- **Recurrent Neural Networks (RNNs)**: Designed for sequential data, RNNs have connections that form directed cycles, allowing information to persist, making them suitable for tasks such as language modeling and time-series prediction. Long Short-Term Memory (LSTM) and Gated Recurrent Unit (GRU) are popular RNN architectures that address the vanishing gradient problem.

- **Generative Adversarial Networks (GANs)**: GANs consist of two neural networks, a generator and a discriminator, that compete against each other. The generator creates fake data, while the discriminator tries to distinguish between real and fake data. This adversarial process improves the generator's ability to produce realistic data. GANs are used in applications like image synthesis, video generation, and style transfer.

2.3 Emerging Techniques and Trends

As ML and DL continue to evolve, several emerging techniques and trends are shaping the future of these fields:

- **Transfer Learning**: This technique involves transferring the knowledge gained from one problem to a different but related problem. It allows models to be trained more efficiently with less data, which is beneficial in scenarios where labeled data is scarce.

- **Few-Shot and Zero-Shot Learning**: Few-shot learning aims to build models that can learn new tasks with very few training examples. Zero-shot learning goes a step further by enabling models to perform tasks they have never seen before. These approaches are crucial for creating adaptable AI systems.

- **Explainable AI (XAI)**: As AI systems become more complex, understanding how they make decisions becomes challenging. XAI aims to make AI models more interpretable and transparent, allowing humans to better understand, trust, and manage AI systems.

- **Federated Learning**: This technique allows models to be trained across multiple devices or servers holding local data samples without exchanging the data itself. This approach enhances data privacy and security, making it suitable for applications in healthcare and finance.

- **Self-Supervised Learning**: This approach involves training models on large amounts of unlabeled data by creating pretext tasks that generate labels from the data itself. Self-supervised learning has shown promise in improving the performance of models, especially in natural language processing and computer vision.

2.4 Applications and Case Studies

The advancements in ML and DL have led to transformative applications across various industries:

- **Healthcare**: AI-powered systems are revolutionizing diagnostics, treatment planning, and drug discovery. For example, deep learning models can analyze medical images to detect conditions such as cancer and diabetic retinopathy with high accuracy.

- **Finance**: ML algorithms are used for fraud detection, risk assessment, and algorithmic trading. AI models analyze transaction patterns to identify suspicious activities and predict market trends.

- **Transportation**: Autonomous vehicles rely on deep learning for perception, decision-making, and control. Companies like Tesla and Waymo are at the forefront of developing self-driving cars that promise to make transportation safer and more efficient.

- **Retail**: Recommendation systems, powered by ML, personalize shopping experiences by analyzing customer behavior and preferences. Retailers like Amazon and Netflix use these systems to suggest products and content users will likely enjoy.

- **Entertainment**: AI is transforming the entertainment industry by enabling new forms of content creation and personalization. For instance, deep learning algorithms generate realistic animations, special effects, and even music compositions.

2.5 Future Directions

The future of ML and DL holds immense potential, with several exciting directions on the horizon:

- **Improving Generalization**: Developing models that generalize well across diverse tasks and domains remains a crucial challenge. Research focuses on creating more robust and versatile AI systems.

- **Reducing Data Dependency**: As AI systems often require large amounts of data, reducing this dependency through techniques like few-shot learning, self-supervised learning, and data augmentation is a critical area of exploration.

- **Ethical AI Development**: Ensuring that AI systems are fair, transparent, and accountable is essential. Researchers are working on methods to detect and mitigate biases, enhance interpretability, and establish ethical guidelines for AI development.

- **Human-AI Collaboration**: Enhancing the synergy between humans and AI systems can lead to more effective decision-making and problem-solving. Developing interfaces and tools that facilitate seamless collaboration is an important focus.

- **Quantum Machine Learning**: Integrating quantum computing with ML has the potential to solve complex problems that are currently intractable. Quantum machine learning is an emerging field that aims to leverage the power of quantum computing for AI.

As we continue to push the boundaries of what is possible with machine learning and deep learning, it is crucial to remain mindful of the ethical and societal implications. By fostering responsible AI development and embracing interdisciplinary collaboration, we can unlock the full potential of these technologies to benefit humanity.

In the next chapter, we will explore how AI is transforming healthcare, from personalized medicine to predictive diagnostics, and the exciting possibilities that lie ahead in this vital field.

CHAPTER 3

AI in Healthcare

AI is revolutionizing healthcare, transforming how we diagnose diseases, develop treatments, and deliver patient care. With its ability to analyze vast amounts of data and identify patterns that might be invisible to human clinicians, AI is poised to enhance medical outcomes, reduce costs, and improve the overall quality of healthcare. In this chapter, we will delve into the various applications of AI in healthcare, exploring how this technology is reshaping the industry and what the future holds.

3.1 Personalized Medicine

Personalized medicine, or precision medicine, involves tailoring medical treatment to each patient's individual characteristics. AI plays a crucial role in this approach by analyzing genetic, environmental, and lifestyle data to create personalized treatment plans.

- **Genomics and AI**: AI algorithms can analyze genomic data to identify genetic mutations and predict how patients will respond to specific treatments. Companies like 23andMe and Ancestry use AI to provide insights into genetic predispositions to certain diseases.

- **Predictive Analytics**: AI systems can predict the likelihood of disease onset based on a patient's health history and genetic information. For example, AI models can forecast the risk of developing conditions like diabetes, heart disease, and cancer, enabling early intervention and preventive care.

- **Drug Discovery**: AI accelerates drug discovery by analyzing biological data to identify potential drug candidates. Machine learning models can predict new drugs' effectiveness and potential side effects, significantly reducing the time and cost involved in bringing new treatments to market.

3.2 Predictive Diagnostics

AI is enhancing the accuracy and speed of medical diagnostics, helping clinicians make more informed decisions and improving patient outcomes.

- **Medical Imaging**: Deep learning algorithms can analyze medical images, such as X-rays, MRIs, and CT scans, to detect abnormalities with high precision. AI systems are used to identify conditions like tumors, fractures, and infections, often more accurately than human radiologists.

- **Pathology**: AI-powered tools can examine tissue samples to diagnose diseases such as cancer. Digital pathology, where AI scans and analyzes slides, is becoming more prevalent, enabling pathologists to identify disease markers quickly and accurately.

- **Wearable Devices**: AI algorithms analyze data from wearable devices to monitor vital signs and detect early signs of health issues. For instance, smartwatches equipped with AI can monitor heart rate and detect irregularities, potentially alerting users to seek medical attention before a serious problem arises.

3.3 Treatment Optimization

AI is transforming treatment planning and delivery, making healthcare more effective and efficient.

- **Robotic Surgery**: AI-powered robotic systems assist surgeons in performing complex procedures with greater precision and control. These systems can analyze preoperative data to plan surgeries and execute them with minimal invasiveness, reducing recovery times and improving outcomes.

- **Radiation Therapy**: AI algorithms optimize radiation therapy by accurately targeting tumors while minimizing damage to surrounding healthy tissue. This precision reduces side effects and improves the effectiveness of cancer treatments.

- **Clinical Decision Support**: AI systems provide clinicians with real-time decision support by analyzing patient data and offering evidence-based recommendations. These tools help doctors choose the best treatment options and avoid potential errors.

3.4 Patient Care and Management

AI improves patient care and management by streamlining administrative processes, enhancing patient engagement, and providing personalized support.

- **Electronic Health Records (EHRs)**: AI enhances EHR systems by automating data entry, reducing administrative burden, and identifying critical insights from patient data. Natural language processing (NLP) algorithms can extract relevant information from clinical notes, making it easier for healthcare providers to access and utilize patient information.

- **Virtual Health Assistants**: AI-powered virtual assistants, such as chatbots and voice-activated systems, give patients instant access to medical information and support. These assistants can answer questions, schedule appointments, and offer personalized health advice, improving patient engagement and satisfaction.

- **Chronic Disease Management**: AI systems help manage chronic diseases by continuously monitoring patient health and providing personalized recommendations. For example, AI-driven platforms can help diabetes patients manage their blood sugar levels by analyzing glucose readings and suggesting lifestyle changes.

3.5 Future Prospects

The future of AI in healthcare is full of promise, with several exciting developments on the horizon.

- **Telemedicine and Remote Monitoring**: AI will play a crucial role in telemedicine, enabling remote consultations and continuous patient monitoring. AI-driven tools can analyze data from remote monitoring devices to detect health issues early and provide timely interventions.

- **AI-Driven Research**: AI will accelerate medical research by analyzing large datasets to uncover new insights and correlations. This capability will enhance our understanding of diseases and lead to the development of novel treatments and therapies.

- **Personal Health Assistants**: Advances in AI will create highly personalized health assistants that can provide real-time health monitoring, disease prediction, and wellness coaching. These assistants will empower individuals to take proactive control of their health.

- **Global Health Impact**: AI can potentially improve healthcare access and quality in underserved regions. AI-powered diagnostic tools and telemedicine can bridge the gap in healthcare delivery, providing essential services to remote and low-resource areas.

3.6 Ethical and Regulatory Considerations

Addressing ethical and regulatory challenges is paramount as AI becomes more integrated into healthcare.

- **Data Privacy and Security**: Protecting patient data is crucial. Ensuring that AI systems comply with data privacy regulations and implementing robust security measures to prevent data breaches are essential.

- **Bias and Fairness**: AI systems must be designed to avoid biases that could lead to unequal treatment. Ensuring diversity in training data and implementing fairness measures are necessary to build equitable AI solutions.

- **Regulatory Approval**: AI-driven medical devices and applications must undergo rigorous regulatory scrutiny to ensure their safety and efficacy. Collaborating with regulatory bodies to establish clear guidelines and standards is vital for the responsible deployment of AI in healthcare.

3.7 Conclusion

Integrating AI into healthcare is transforming the industry, offering new possibilities for personalized medicine, predictive diagnostics, and optimized treatment. As AI technologies continue to evolve, they hold the potential to improve patient outcomes, reduce healthcare costs, and enhance the overall quality of care. However, realizing this potential requires careful consideration of ethical, regulatory, and societal implications.

In the next chapter, we will explore AI's impact on autonomous systems, including self-driving cars, drones, and robotics, and how these technologies are reshaping transportation and other industries.

CHAPTER 4

Autonomous Systems

Autonomous systems are transforming industries by introducing new levels of efficiency, safety, and innovation. These systems, which include self-driving cars, drones, and robots, leverage AI to operate independently, make decisions, and perform tasks without human intervention. In this chapter, we will explore autonomous systems' advancements, applications, and future prospects, focusing on their impact on transportation, logistics, agriculture, and beyond.

4.1 Self-Driving Cars

Self-driving cars, also known as autonomous vehicles (AVs), are among the most well-known applications of autonomous systems. These vehicles use a combination of sensors, AI algorithms, and advanced computing to navigate and drive without human input.

- **Technology Behind Self-Driving Cars:**

- **Sensors**: Self-driving cars have various sensors, including LIDAR (Light Detection and Ranging), radar, cameras, and ultrasonic sensors. These sensors provide real-time data about the car's surroundings, enabling it to detect obstacles, pedestrians, and other vehicles.

- **AI and Machine Learning**: AI algorithms process sensor data to make driving decisions. Machine learning models are trained on vast amounts of driving data to recognize patterns and predict the behavior of other road users.

- **Mapping and Localization**: High-definition maps and GPS technology help autonomous vehicles navigate and stay on course. Localization techniques ensure the vehicle knows its exact position on the road.

- **Levels of Autonomy**: The Society of Automotive Engineers (SAE) defines six levels of vehicle autonomy, from Level 0 (no automation) to Level 5 (full automation). Most current autonomous vehicles operate at Level 2 or 3, which involve partial automation with driver supervision. Level 4 and 5 vehicles, capable of full self-driving without human intervention, are in development and testing.

- **Benefits and Challenges**:

- **Benefits**: Autonomous vehicles have the potential to reduce traffic accidents, decrease congestion, and provide mobility solutions for people with disabilities or those unable to drive.

- **Challenges**: Technical challenges include ensuring safety and reliability in diverse driving conditions. Regulatory and legal hurdles, such as liability and insurance issues, must be addressed. Public acceptance and trust in autonomous technology are also crucial.

4.2 Drones

Drones, or unmanned aerial vehicles (UAVs), are transforming industries by providing new aerial surveillance, delivery, and data collection capabilities.

- **Types of Drones:**

- **Consumer Drones**: Typically used for recreational purposes, photography, and videography.

- **Commercial Drones**: Used in industries such as agriculture, construction, and logistics for tasks like crop monitoring, infrastructure inspection, and package delivery.

- **Military Drones**: Employed for surveillance, reconnaissance, and combat missions.

- **Applications of Drones:**

- **Agriculture**: Drones equipped with multispectral sensors monitor crop health, optimize irrigation, and apply pesticides with precision.

- **Logistics and Delivery**: Companies like Amazon and UPS are exploring drone delivery systems to provide faster and more efficient package delivery.

- **Disaster Response**: Drones assist in search and rescue operations, damage assessment, and delivering supplies to inaccessible areas.

- **Infrastructure Inspection**: Drones inspect bridges, power lines, and pipelines, reducing the need for manual inspections and improving safety.

- **Regulatory and Ethical Considerations**:

- **Regulations**: Ensuring safe and legal drone operations requires adherence to regulations set by aviation authorities, such as the Federal Aviation Administration (FAA) in the United States.

- **Privacy and Security**: Addressing privacy concerns related to drone surveillance and protecting against potential misuse are critical issues.

4.3 Robotics

Robotics is a broad field that encompasses the design, construction, and operation of robots. Robots are increasingly used in manufacturing, healthcare, service industries, and other industries.

- **Industrial Robots**:

- **Manufacturing**: Industrial robots automate tasks such as assembly, welding, painting, and packaging, improving efficiency and precision in manufacturing processes.

- **Collaborative Robots (Cobots)**: Cobots work alongside human workers, assisting with tasks that require flexibility and adaptability. They are designed to be safe and easy to program, making them suitable for small and medium-sized enterprises.

- **Service Robots**:

- **Healthcare**: Robots assist in surgeries, rehabilitation, and patient care. Surgical robots, like the Da Vinci system, provide surgeons with enhanced precision and control.

- **Hospitality**: Robots are used in hotels and restaurants to deliver room service, clean, and interact with customers.

- **Humanoid Robots**: Humanoid robots mimic human movements and interactions, making them suitable for applications in customer service, education, and entertainment.

- **Future Trends in Robotics**:

- **Advancements in AI**: Integrating AI with robotics enables more intelligent and autonomous robots capable of learning from experience and adapting to new tasks.

- **Swarm Robotics:** Inspired by the behavior of social insects, swarm robotics involves multiple robots working together to accomplish complex tasks, such as search and rescue missions or agricultural operations.

- **Soft Robotics:** Soft robots are made from flexible materials, allowing them to interact safely with humans and adapt to unpredictable environments. They are particularly useful in delicate tasks, such as handling soft fruits or performing minimally invasive surgeries.

4.4 Impact on Transportation and Logistics

Autonomous systems are revolutionizing transportation and logistics, bringing significant benefits and challenges.

- **Efficient Transportation:**

- **Public Transit:** Autonomous buses and shuttles can enhance public transportation systems by providing more reliable and efficient services.

- **Freight and Logistics:** Self-driving trucks and delivery drones can optimize supply chains, reduce delivery times, and lower costs. Companies like Tesla and Waymo are developing autonomous trucks that can operate continuously, increasing efficiency in freight transportation.

- **Last-Mile Delivery:** Autonomous delivery robots and drones can solve the last-mile delivery challenge, providing quick and cost-effective solutions for urban deliveries.

- **Sustainability**: Autonomous systems can contribute to sustainability by optimizing routes, reducing fuel consumption, and minimizing emissions. Electric autonomous vehicles, in particular, offer a cleaner alternative to traditional fossil-fuel-powered transportation.

4.5 Ethical and Social Implications

The rise of autonomous systems raises important ethical and social questions that must be addressed.

- **Job Displacement**: Automating tasks traditionally performed by humans may lead to job displacement in transportation, logistics, manufacturing, and other industries. To mitigate these impacts, workforce retraining and education strategies must be considered.

- **Safety and Liability**: Ensuring the safety of autonomous systems is paramount. Developing robust safety protocols, establishing clear liability frameworks, and gaining public trust are critical.

- **Privacy Concerns**: Autonomous systems, particularly drones and surveillance robots, can pose privacy risks. Strict privacy regulations and transparency in data collection and usage must be implemented to protect individuals' privacy rights,

- **Ethical Decision-Making**: Autonomous systems must be programmed to make ethical decisions, especially in critical situations such as avoiding accidents. Establishing ethical guidelines and frameworks for AI decision-making is crucial.

4.6 Conclusion

Autonomous systems are at the forefront of technological innovation, transforming industries and reshaping our world. From self-driving cars to drones and robots, these systems offer numerous benefits, including increased efficiency, safety, and sustainability. However, realizing the full potential of autonomous systems requires addressing technical, regulatory, ethical, and social challenges.

In the next chapter, we will explore the advancements in natural language processing (NLP), a critical area of AI that enables machines to understand and interact with human language. We will also examine NLP's applications in various domains and its future prospects.

CHAPTER 5

Natural Language Processing (NLP)

Natural Language Processing (NLP) is a critical area of AI that focuses on the interaction between computers and human language. NLP enables machines to understand, interpret, and generate human language in a meaningful and useful way. This chapter explores the key concepts, techniques, and applications of NLP, its future prospects, and its challenges.

5.1 Fundamentals of Natural Language Processing

NLP combines computational linguistics with machine learning and deep learning to process and analyze large amounts of natural language data. Its primary goal is to enable computers to perform tasks involving human language, such as translation, sentiment analysis, and question answering.

- **Key Components of NLP:**

- **Tokenization**: Breaking down text into smaller units, such as words or phrases, known as tokens.

- **Part-of-Speech Tagging**: Identifying the grammatical categories (e.g., nouns, verbs, adjectives) of each token in a sentence.

- **Named Entity Recognition (NER)**: Detecting and classifying named entities (e.g., people, organizations, locations) within text.

- **Parsing**: Analyzing the grammatical structure of a sentence to understand its meaning.

- **Sentiment Analysis**: Determining the sentiment expressed in a text, whether positive, negative, or neutral.

- **Machine Translation**: Automatically translating text from one language to another.

- **Text Summarization**: Condensing a large body of text into a shorter version while retaining key information.

- **Speech Recognition**: Converting spoken language into written text.

5.2 Techniques in Natural Language Processing

NLP relies on various techniques, from traditional linguistic methods to advanced machine learning and deep learning approaches.

- **Rule-Based Methods**: Early NLP systems used hand-crafted rules based on linguistic knowledge to process language. While these methods are straightforward, they often struggle with the complexity and variability of natural language.

- **Statistical Methods**: With the advent of machine learning, statistical methods became popular in NLP. These methods use probabilistic models to learn from large datasets and make predictions about language.

- **Neural Networks and Deep Learning**: Deep learning has revolutionized NLP by enabling models to learn complex patterns and representations from large amounts of data. Key architectures include:

- **Recurrent Neural Networks (RNNs)**: Suitable for sequential data, RNNs are used for tasks such as language modeling and machine translation. Variants like Long Short-Term Memory (LSTM) and Gated Recurrent Unit (GRU) address the vanishing gradient problem in RNNs.

- **Convolutional Neural Networks (CNNs)**: Although primarily used in image processing, CNNs have been adapted for NLP tasks like text classification.

- **Transformers**: The transformer architecture has become the foundation for many state-of-the-art NLP models. Transformers use self-attention mechanisms to process entire sentences simultaneously, enabling efficient parallelization and improved performance. Models like BERT (Bidirectional Encoder Representations from Transformers) and GPT (Generative Pre-trained Transformer) are based on this architecture.

5.3 Applications of NLP

NLP is transforming various industries by enabling new and improved ways of interacting with language data.

- **Virtual Assistants and Chatbots**: NLP powers virtual assistants like Siri, Alexa, and Google Assistant, enabling them to understand and respond to user queries. Chatbots are used in customer service to provide instant support and automate routine tasks.

- **Translation Services**: Machine translation systems, such as Google Translate, use NLP to translate text between languages, breaking down language barriers and facilitating global communication.

- **Content Generation**: NLP models can generate human-like text, enabling applications such as automated news writing, content summarization, and creative writing. Tools like OpenAI's GPT-3 can produce coherent and contextually relevant text based on prompts.

- **Sentiment Analysis**: Businesses use sentiment analysis to gauge customer opinions and feedback from social media, reviews, and surveys. This analysis helps companies understand customer satisfaction and improve their products and services.

- **Information Retrieval**: NLP enhances search engines and recommendation systems by improving their ability to understand and retrieve relevant information based on user queries. Doing so is critical for applications like document retrieval, e-commerce, and personalized content recommendations.

- **Healthcare**: NLP analyzes clinical notes, extracts relevant information from medical records, and assists in medical research. NLP tools can also help in patient interaction through virtual health assistants.

5.4 Future Prospects

The future of NLP holds immense potential as research and development continue to advance the field.

- **Improved Understanding and Context**: Future NLP systems will better understand context, enabling more accurate and nuanced language processing. This includes understanding idiomatic expressions, cultural references, and complex sentence structures.

- **Multimodal NLP**: Combining NLP with other AI domains, such as computer vision and speech recognition, will enable systems to process and generate multimodal content. For example, AI could analyze videos by understanding spoken language and visual content.

- **Personalization and Adaptation**: NLP systems will become more personalized, adapting to individual user preferences and communication styles, thus enhancing user experiences in applications like virtual assistants, chatbots, and recommendation systems.

- **Ethical and Responsible NLP**: Ensuring that NLP systems are fair, transparent, and free from bias is a critical area of focus. Researchers are working on methods to detect and mitigate biases in NLP models and to make these systems more interpretable and accountable.

- **Low-Resource Languages**: Advances in NLP will enable the development of robust language processing tools for low-resource languages, which currently lack large datasets and linguistic resources. This development will democratize access to NLP technologies and promote linguistic diversity.

5.5 Challenges and Considerations

Despite the progress in NLP, several challenges and considerations must be addressed.

- **Bias and Fairness**: NLP models trained on biased data can perpetuate and amplify biases. Ensuring fairness and addressing bias in NLP systems is crucial to prevent discriminatory outcomes.

- **Data Privacy**: Protecting user data and ensuring privacy in NLP applications, especially those involving sensitive information, is a significant concern. Developing privacy-preserving techniques is essential for ethical NLP.

- **Interpretability**: As NLP models become more complex, understanding how they make decisions becomes challenging. Improving their interpretability is essential for building trust and ensuring responsible use.

- **Language Diversity**: Many NLP advancements are focused on a few dominant languages. Expanding NLP research to include more languages and dialects is necessary for creating inclusive and equitable language technologies.

- **Resource Requirements**: Training large NLP models requires significant computational resources and energy, raising concerns about sustainability and accessibility. Developing more efficient models and techniques is essential for addressing these challenges.

5.6 Conclusion

Natural Language Processing is a transformative field that enables machines to understand and interact with human language. From virtual assistants and translation services to content generation and sentiment analysis, NLP is reshaping industries and improving our interactions with technology. As research advances, the future of NLP promises even more sophisticated and personalized language processing capabilities. However, addressing ethical, fairness, and resource challenges is crucial to ensuring that NLP technologies benefit all of humanity.

In the next chapter, we will explore AI's ethical and responsible development, examining the principles and practices that guide the creation of fair, transparent, and accountable AI systems.

CHAPTER 6

Ethical and Responsible AI

As AI becomes increasingly integrated into various aspects of society, it brings tremendous benefits and significant ethical challenges. The development and deployment of AI systems raise questions about fairness, transparency, accountability, and the impact on society. In this chapter, we will explore the principles and practices that guide AI's ethical and responsible development, addressing issues such as bias, privacy, safety, and the future implications of AI technologies.

6.1 Understanding AI Ethics

AI ethics involves the moral implications and societal impacts of AI technologies. It encompasses a range of issues, including:

- **Fairness and Bias**: Ensuring that AI systems treat all individuals and groups fairly and do not perpetuate or amplify existing biases.

- **Transparency**: Making AI systems understandable and interpretable will allow users to trust and comprehend how decisions are made.

- **Accountability**: Establishing clear lines of responsibility for the actions and outcomes of AI systems.

- **Privacy**: Protecting individuals' personal data and privacy in the design and operation of AI systems.

- **Safety**: Ensuring that AI systems operate reliably and do not pose risks to human safety and well-being.

6.2 Addressing Bias and Fairness

One of AI's most pressing ethical challenges is addressing bias and ensuring fairness. AI systems can inadvertently learn and propagate biases present in their training data, leading to discriminatory outcomes.

- **Sources of Bias**: Bias can arise from various sources, including biased training data, biased algorithms, and biased human decision-making. Identifying and mitigating these sources is essential to ensure fair AI systems.

- **Mitigation Strategies**:

- **Diverse and Representative Data**: Using diverse and representative datasets for training AI models can help reduce bias. Ensuring that data includes various demographic groups and perspectives is crucial.

- **Algorithmic Fairness**: Developing algorithms incorporating fairness constraints and regularization techniques can help mitigate bias. Techniques like re-weighting, re-sampling, and adversarial debiasing are commonly used.

- **Bias Audits and Testing**: Regularly auditing and testing AI systems for bias can help identify and address issues before deployment. These processes involve evaluating the system's performance across different demographic groups and scenarios.

6.3 Ensuring Transparency and Interpretability

Transparency and interpretability are critical for building trust in AI systems. Users must understand how AI systems make decisions to ensure accountability and address potential issues.

- **Explainable AI (XAI)**: Explainable AI aims to make AI models more interpretable and transparent. Techniques such as model simplification, feature importance analysis, and local explanations (e.g., LIME, SHAP) help provide insights into how models make decisions.

- **Human-in-the-Loop**: Incorporating human oversight in AI decision-making can enhance transparency and accountability. This approach ensures that humans can intervene and provide context when necessary.

- **Clear Documentation**: Providing clear and comprehensive documentation of AI models, including their development, data sources, and decision-making processes, helps users understand and trust the systems.

6.4 Accountability in AI Systems

Accountability in AI involves establishing clear responsibilities for the actions and outcomes of AI systems and determining who is responsible for the design, deployment, and impact of AI technologies.

- **Legal and Regulatory Frameworks**: It is crucial to develop legal and regulatory frameworks that define accountability and liability for AI systems. Such measures would include addressing issues such as liability for harm caused by AI and ensuring compliance with ethical standards.

- **Ethical Guidelines and Standards**: Establishing ethical guidelines and industry standards can help ensure responsible AI development. Organizations such as the IEEE, the European Commission, and the Partnership on AI have developed procedures to promote ethical AI practices.

- **Internal Governance**: Implementing internal governance structures within organizations can help ensure accountability. This includes creating ethics committees, appointing ethics officers, and establishing clear policies and procedures for ethical AI development.

6.5 Protecting Privacy

AI systems often rely on large amounts of personal data, raising privacy and data protection concerns. Ensuring that AI systems respect privacy rights is essential for ethical AI development.

- **Data Minimization**: Collecting and using only the minimum amount of data necessary for AI tasks can help protect privacy. Data minimization principles ensure that unnecessary data is not collected or retained.

- **Anonymization and De-identification**: Techniques such as anonymization and de-identification can help protect individuals' privacy by removing personally identifiable information from datasets.

- **Privacy-Preserving Techniques**: Advanced techniques such as differential privacy, federated learning, and secure multi-party computation enable AI models to learn from data while preserving privacy. These techniques protect individual data points, even when aggregated insights are derived.

6.6 Ensuring Safety and Reliability

Ensuring the safety and reliability of AI systems is paramount, especially in critical applications such as healthcare, transportation, and finance.

- **Robustness and Resilience**: AI systems should be designed to be robust and resilient to errors, adversarial attacks, and unexpected inputs. Techniques such as adversarial training, robustness testing, and redundancy can enhance the reliability of AI systems.

- **Continuous Monitoring**: Implementing constant monitoring and evaluation of AI systems in real-world environments helps identify and address issues promptly. This includes tracking system performance, detecting anomalies, and implementing feedback loops.

- **Safety Standards**: Developing and adhering to safety standards and best practices in AI development can help ensure that AI systems operate reliably and safely. Standards organizations such as ISO and IEEE provide guidelines for safety-critical AI applications.

6.7 Ethical Implications of Future AI Technologies

As AI technologies evolve, they bring new ethical implications that must be addressed proactively.

- **Autonomous Systems**: Deploying autonomous systems, such as self-driving cars and drones, raises ethical questions about decision-making in critical situations, liability for accidents, and the impact on employment.

- **AI in Warfare**: Using AI in military applications, including autonomous weapons, poses significant ethical and moral questions. Ensuring that AI is used responsibly in warfare and complies with international humanitarian law is essential.

- **Human-AI Collaboration**: As AI systems become more integrated into daily life, it is crucial to ensure that humans and AI collaborate effectively and ethically. This includes addressing issues of autonomy, trust, and the balance of control between humans and machines.

6.8 Conclusion

Ethical and responsible AI development ensures that AI technologies benefit society while minimizing risks and harms. By addressing issues of bias, transparency, accountability, privacy, and safety, we can build AI systems that are fair, trustworthy, and aligned with human values. As AI continues to advance, proactive efforts to address ethical challenges and establish robust governance frameworks will be crucial for shaping AI's positive and inclusive future.

In the next chapter, we will explore the role of AI in education and workforce development, examining how AI is transforming learning experiences and preparing individuals for the jobs of the future.

CHAPTER 7

AI in Education and Workforce Development

AI is reshaping education and workforce development by providing personalized learning experiences, enhancing educational tools, and preparing individuals for the jobs of the future. This chapter explores how AI transforms education, from personalized learning and intelligent tutoring systems to skills training and lifelong learning. We will also discuss the implications of AI for workforce development and the strategies needed to prepare for an AI-driven economy.

7.1 Personalized Learning

Personalized learning tailors educational experiences to individual students' needs, preferences, and learning styles. AI is crucial in creating adaptive learning environments that cater to each student.

- **Adaptive Learning Platforms**: AI-driven adaptive learning platforms analyze students' interactions and performance data to provide customized learning paths. These platforms adjust the difficulty level, pace, and content based on the student's progress, ensuring they are energized and engaged.

- **Intelligent Tutoring Systems (ITS)**: ITS uses AI to provide one-on-one tutoring and feedback to students. These systems can identify areas where students struggle and offer targeted assistance, mimicking the personalized attention of a human tutor.

- **Learning Analytics**: AI-powered learning analytics tools track and analyze student data to provide insights into learning patterns, identify at-risk students, and suggest interventions. Educators can use these insights to tailor instruction and improve student outcomes.

7.2 Enhancing Educational Tools and Resources

AI enhances educational tools and resources, making them more effective, interactive, and accessible.

- **Content Creation and Curation**: AI can generate and curate educational content, such as quizzes, practice exercises, and multimedia resources, helping educators save time and providing students with a diverse array of learning materials.

- **Virtual Classrooms and Online Learning**: AI-powered virtual classrooms and online learning platforms offer interactive and engaging learning experiences. Features like automated grading, discussion moderation, and personalized recommendations enhance the online learning environment.

- **Language Learning**: AI-driven language learning apps, such as Duolingo and Babbel, use machine learning to provide personalized lessons, instant feedback, and language practice tailored to each learner's proficiency level.

7.3 Preparing for an AI-Driven Workforce

AI is transforming the job market, creating new opportunities and challenges for workforce development. Preparing individuals for an AI-driven economy requires a focus on skills training, reskilling, and lifelong learning.

- **Skills Training and Reskilling**: As AI automates routine tasks, there is a growing demand for skills that complement AI, such as critical thinking, creativity, and emotional intelligence. AI-powered training platforms can provide personalized skill development and reskilling programs to help individuals adapt to changing job requirements.

- **Lifelong Learning**: In an AI-driven economy, continuous learning is essential. AI can support lifelong learning by offering personalized learning paths, recommending relevant courses, and providing opportunities for hands-on practice and real-world application.

- **Career Guidance and Planning**: AI-driven career guidance tools analyze labor market trends, individual skills, and career goals to provide personalized career recommendations. These tools can help individuals identify emerging job opportunities and plan their career trajectories.

7.4 AI in Higher Education

Higher education institutions leverage AI to enhance learning experiences, improve administrative processes, and support student success.

- **Student Admissions and Enrollment**: AI can streamline the admissions process by analyzing applications, predicting student success, and identifying the best-fit candidates. Institutions can then make data-driven decisions and improve enrollment outcomes.

- **Academic Advising**: AI-powered academic advising systems provide personalized support to students, helping them select courses, plan their educational paths, and stay on track for graduation. These systems can identify at-risk students and suggest interventions to improve retention and success rates.

- **Research and Innovation**: AI supports research by automating data analysis, identifying patterns, and generating insights. Researchers can use AI tools to enhance their work, collaborate more effectively, and accelerate innovation.

7.5 AI in K-12 Education

AI is also making significant strides in K-12 education, enhancing teaching and learning at the primary and secondary levels.

- **Classroom Management**: AI-driven classroom management tools help teachers monitor student behavior, track attendance, and manage classroom activities. These tools can identify students who need additional support and provide real-time feedback to educators.

- **Special Education**: AI can support special education by providing personalized learning plans, assistive technologies, and adaptive learning tools for students with disabilities, ensuring that all students have access to quality education and can achieve their full potential.

- **Parental Engagement**: AI-powered communication platforms facilitate better communication between teachers, parents, and students. These platforms provide updates on student progress, share resources, and enable parents to be more involved in their child's education.

7.6 Ethical Considerations in AI-Driven Education

As AI becomes more integrated into education, ethical considerations must be addressed to ensure that its benefits are realized equitably and responsibly.

- **Equity and Access**: It is crucial to ensure that all students have access to AI-driven educational tools and resources. Addressing the digital divide and supporting underserved communities can help bridge gaps in access and opportunity.

- **Data Privacy**: Protecting student data and ensuring privacy is paramount. Educational institutions must implement robust data protection measures and comply with privacy regulations to safeguard student information.

- **Bias and Fairness**: AI systems must be designed to be fair and unbiased. This objective can be accomplished by using diverse and representative data, continuously monitoring for bias, and implementing fairness constraints in AI models.

- **Human Oversight**: While AI can enhance education, human oversight is essential to ensure that AI-driven decisions are appropriate and ethical. Educators and administrators must remain actively involved in implementing and using AI technologies.

7.7 Conclusion

AI is transforming education and workforce development, offering new possibilities for personalized learning, skills training, and lifelong learning. By leveraging AI, educational institutions can enhance teaching and learning experiences, improve administrative processes, and better prepare individuals for the jobs of the future. However, addressing ethical considerations and ensuring that AI is used responsibly and equitably is essential.

In the next chapter, we will explore the integration of AI with the Internet of Things (IoT) and edge computing, examining how these technologies create more innovative and responsive environments across various industries.

CHAPTER 8

Integration with IoT and Edge Computing

Integrating AI with the Internet of Things (IoT) and edge computing creates more innovative and responsive environments across various industries. This convergence enables real-time data processing, enhanced decision-making, and improved efficiency in areas such as smart cities, industrial automation, healthcare, and agriculture. In this chapter, we will examine IoT and edge computing, their integration with AI, and the transformative impact of this synergy.

8.1 Understanding IoT and Edge Computing

The Internet of Things (IoT) refers to a network of interconnected devices that collect, share, and analyze data through the internet. These devices range from everyday household items to industrial machinery equipped with sensors and communication capabilities.

- **Components of IoT**:

- **Sensors**: Devices that detect and measure physical properties such as temperature, humidity, motion, and light.

- **Connectivity**: Networks that enable communication between IoT devices and centralized systems, including Wi-Fi, Bluetooth, cellular, and satellite connections.

- **Data Processing**: Systems that analyze data collected by IoT devices to extract meaningful insights and trigger actions.

Edge computing brings data processing closer to the source of data generation, reducing latency and bandwidth usage. By performing computations at the network's edge, closer to the IoT devices, edge computing enables faster and more efficient data processing.

- **Key Benefits of Edge Computing**:

- **Reduced Latency**: Processing data locally minimizes the time it takes to analyze and respond to data, enabling real-time decision-making.

- **Bandwidth Optimization**: Edge computing reduces the amount of data transmitted to central servers, optimizing bandwidth usage and lowering costs.

- **Enhanced Security**: Local data processing can improve security by minimizing data exposure and reducing the risk of data breaches during transmission.

8.2 The Convergence of AI, IoT, and Edge Computing

Integrating AI with IoT and edge computing combines the strengths of these technologies, resulting in intelligent systems capable of real-time analysis and decision-making.

- **AI-Enhanced IoT**: AI algorithms can analyze vast amounts of data generated by IoT devices to identify patterns, make predictions, and optimize operations. This integration enables more efficient and intelligent IoT systems.

- **Edge AI**: Deploying AI models at the network's edge allows for real-time data processing and decision-making without relying on centralized cloud services. Edge AI enhances the responsiveness and efficiency of IoT applications.

8.3 Applications of AI, IoT, and Edge Computing

Integrating AI, IoT, and edge computing is transforming various industries by enabling innovative applications and improving existing processes.

- **Smart Cities**:

- **Traffic Management**: AI-powered traffic management systems use data from IoT sensors and cameras to monitor traffic flow, optimize signal timings, and reduce congestion. Real-time analysis helps manage traffic incidents and improve overall transportation efficiency.

- **Energy Management**: Smart grids use AI and IoT to monitor and optimize energy consumption, balance supply and demand, and integrate renewable energy sources, leading to more efficient and sustainable energy usage in urban environments.

- **Public Safety**: AI-driven surveillance systems analyze data from IoT cameras and sensors to detect anomalies, identify potential threats, and enhance public safety. Edge computing enables real-time analysis and rapid response.

- **Industrial Automation**:

- **Predictive Maintenance**: AI algorithms analyze data from IoT sensors on industrial equipment to predict failures and schedule maintenance before issues occur, reducing downtime and maintenance costs and improving overall productivity.

- **Process Optimization**: IoT devices monitor and control industrial processes, while AI models analyze data to optimize operations, reduce waste, and improve quality. Edge computing ensures real-time adjustments and efficient process control.

- **Supply Chain Management**: AI and IoT enable real-time tracking and management of supply chains. Sensors monitor the condition and location of goods, while AI analyzes data to optimize logistics, reduce delays, and improve inventory management.

- **Healthcare:**

- **Remote Patient Monitoring:** IoT devices collect health data from patients, which AI models analyze to detect abnormalities and provide early warnings. Edge computing enables real-time monitoring and immediate interventions, improving patient outcomes.

- **Smart Medical Devices:** AI-enhanced medical devices, such as insulin pumps and cardiac monitors, use real-time data analysis to adjust treatments and provide personalized care. Edge computing ensures quick and reliable device operation.

- **Operational Efficiency:** IoT sensors and AI analytics optimize hospital operations by monitoring equipment usage, managing inventory, and improving patient flow, leading to better resource utilization and enhanced patient care.

- **Agriculture:**

- **Precision Farming:** IoT sensors collect data on soil conditions, weather, and crop health, while AI analyzes this data to optimize irrigation, fertilization, and pest control. Edge computing ensures real-time adjustments and efficient resource use.

- **Livestock Monitoring**: IoT devices track livestock health and behavior, and AI models analyze data to detect signs of illness and optimize feeding schedules, improving animal welfare and farm productivity.

- **Supply Chain Optimization**: AI and IoT enable real-time tracking and management of agricultural supply chains, reducing waste, improving logistics, and ensuring the freshness of produce.

8.4 Future Trends and Challenges

Integrating AI, IoT, and edge computing is poised to drive further innovation and transformation across industries. However, several trends and challenges need to be addressed to realize the full potential of these technologies.

- **5G Connectivity**: The rollout of 5G networks will enhance the capabilities of IoT and edge computing by providing faster, more reliable connectivity. This rollout will enable more devices to connect and communicate in real time, enhancing AI-driven applications.

- **Edge Intelligence**: Advancements in edge AI will enable more sophisticated data processing and decision-making at the network's edge. These advancements include the development of lightweight AI models that can run on resource-constrained edge devices.

- **Interoperability and Standards**: Ensuring interoperability between different IoT devices and platforms is crucial for seamless integration and scalability. Developing and adopting industry standards will facilitate this process.

- **Security and Privacy**: Protecting data privacy and ensuring the security of IoT devices and edge computing systems are paramount. Implementing robust security measures and adhering to privacy regulations are essential to mitigate risks.

- **Scalability and Management**: Managing and scaling IoT and edge computing infrastructure can be complex. Developing efficient management and orchestration tools will be critical to handle large-scale deployments.

8.5 Ethical Considerations

As AI, IoT, and edge computing become more pervasive, addressing ethical considerations is essential to ensure responsible and equitable use of these technologies.

- **Data Privacy**: Protecting the privacy of individuals' data collected by IoT devices is crucial. Implementing data anonymization, encryption, and access control measures can help safeguard privacy.

- **Bias and Fairness**: AI models used in IoT applications must be designed to avoid bias and ensure fairness. This involves using diverse datasets, monitoring for biases, and implementing fairness constraints.

- **Environmental Impact**: The proliferation of IoT devices and edge computing infrastructure has environmental implications, such as increased energy consumption and electronic waste. Developing energy-efficient technologies and promoting recycling and sustainability practices are essential.

8.6 Conclusion

Integrating AI with IoT and edge computing creates intelligent and responsive environments that enhance efficiency, decision-making, and innovation across various industries. We can build smarter cities, optimize industrial processes, improve healthcare, and advance agriculture by leveraging these technologies. However, addressing technical, ethical, and regulatory challenges is essential to ensure the responsible and equitable use of AI, IoT, and edge computing.

In the next chapter, we will explore how AI is influencing creativity and art, examining its role in generating music, visual art, literature, and other creative works and discussing its implications for artists and the creative industry.

CHAPTER 9

AI in Creativity and Art

AI is making significant inroads into creativity and art, transforming how we create, experience, and appreciate artistic works. From generating music and visual art to writing literature and enhancing creative processes, AI is becoming an invaluable tool for artists and creators. In this chapter, we will explore the various applications of AI in creativity and art, the technologies driving these innovations, and the implications for artists and the creative industry.

9.1 AI in Music

AI is revolutionizing the music industry by assisting in composition, performance, and production. AI algorithms analyze vast amounts of musical data to generate new compositions, suggest harmonies, and even create entirely new genres of music.

- **Music Composition**: AI tools like OpenAI's MuseNet and Google's Magenta project can generate original music by learning from large datasets of existing compositions.

These tools can compose in various styles and genres, from classical to jazz to electronic music.

- **Assistive Tools for Musicians**: AI-driven software, such as Amper Music and AIVA, assists musicians by suggesting chord progressions, harmonies, and melodies. These tools can enhance the creative process by providing new ideas and inspiration.

- **Music Production**: AI is used in music production to automate tasks such as mixing, mastering, and sound design. AI algorithms analyze audio tracks and apply effects, equalization, and compression to produce high-quality recordings.

9.2 AI in Visual Art

AI is also making waves in visual art, enabling the creation of new artworks, enhancing existing ones, and providing artists with novel tools for expression.

- **Generative Art**: Generative Adversarial Networks (GANs), such as those used by the DeepArt and Artbreeder platforms, can create stunning visual art by learning from a dataset of images and generating new ones that mimic the styles of famous artists or inventing entirely new styles.

- **Style Transfer**: AI algorithms can apply the style of one image to another, creating unique artworks that blend different visual elements. This technique, known as style transfer, has been popularized by tools like DeepArt and Prisma.

- **AI-Assisted Design**: Tools like Adobe's Sensei and Autodesk's Dreamcatcher use AI to assist designers by suggesting layouts, color schemes, and design elements. These tools can enhance the creative process by providing new perspectives and possibilities.

9.3 AI in Literature

AI is also influencing the field of literature, from generating text and assisting in writing to analyzing literary works and providing new insights.

- **Text Generation**: AI models like OpenAI's GPT-3 can generate human-like text based on prompts, enabling the creation of stories, poems, and articles. These models can mimic the style of various authors and create coherent and contextually relevant narratives.

- **Writing Assistance**: AI-powered writing tools, such as Grammarly and ProWritingAid, assist writers by providing suggestions for grammar, style, and tone. These tools can improve the quality of writing and help authors refine their work.

- **Literary Analysis**: AI algorithms can analyze literary texts to identify themes, motifs, and stylistic elements, providing new insights into literary works and helping scholars and critics explore texts in greater depth.

9.4 AI in Film and Animation

AI is transforming the film and animation industry by enhancing special effects, automating editing processes, and generating scripts.

- **Special Effects**: AI-driven tools create realistic special effects, such as de-aging actors, generating realistic environments, and enhancing visual effects. AI algorithms can analyze footage and apply effects with high precision, reducing the need for manual intervention.

- **Automated Editing**: AI-powered editing software, like Adobe Premiere Pro's Auto Reframe, automates the editing process by analyzing footage and making intelligent cuts and transitions. This saves editors time and improves the efficiency of the post-production process.

- **Scriptwriting**: AI tools can assist in scriptwriting by generating dialogue, suggesting plot points, and providing story ideas. While AI-generated scripts are not yet on par with human-written ones, they can serve as a valuable resource for writers looking for inspiration.

9.5 The Implications of AI in Creativity and Art

Integrating AI into the creative process has profound implications for artists, the creative industry, and society as a whole.

- **Empowering Artists**: AI tools can empower artists by providing new creative possibilities, enhancing their skills, and enabling them to explore new styles and techniques. These tools can serve as collaborators, rather than replacements, for human creativity.

- **Redefining Creativity**: Using AI in art challenges traditional notions of creativity and authorship. Questions arise about the artist's role, the nature of creativity, and the value of AI-generated art. These discussions can lead to a broader understanding of what it means to be creative.

- **Economic Impact**: AI can democratize access to creative tools, enabling more people to create art and participate in the creative economy. However, it also raises concerns about job displacement in the creative industry and the potential devaluation of human-made art.

- **Ethical Considerations**: The use of AI in art raises ethical questions about copyright, ownership, and the potential for misuse. Ensuring that AI-generated art respects intellectual property rights and ethical standards is essential.

9.6 Future Prospects

The future of AI in creativity and art holds exciting possibilities as technology continues to advance and artists explore new ways to integrate AI into their work.

- **Collaborative AI**: Future AI systems will be designed to collaborate more seamlessly with human artists, providing real-time feedback and suggestions while preserving the artist's creative vision.

- **Multimodal Art**: The convergence of AI with other technologies, such as virtual reality (VR) and augmented reality (AR), will enable the creation of immersive and interactive art experiences that blend visual, auditory, and tactile elements.

- **Enhanced Creativity**: Advances in AI will lead to more sophisticated creative tools that can understand and respond to an artist's unique style and preferences, enhancing their creative process and enabling new forms of artistic expression.

9.7 Conclusion

AI is transforming the world of creativity and art, providing artists with powerful tools for expression and enabling the creation of new and innovative works. From music and visual art to literature and film, AI is reshaping the creative landscape and challenging our understanding of creativity. As AI continues to evolve, it will open up new possibilities for artistic exploration and collaboration while raising important questions about the nature of creativity and the role of technology in the creative process.

In the next chapter, we will explore the applications of AI in finance and business, examining how AI is revolutionizing financial services, enhancing business processes, and driving data-driven decision-making.

CHAPTER 10

AI in Finance and Business

AI is revolutionizing the finance and business sectors by enhancing efficiency, improving decision-making, and providing innovative solutions to complex problems. From fraud detection and risk management to personalized financial services and automated business processes, AI is transforming how organizations operate and compete. In this chapter, we will explore the various applications of AI in finance and business, the technologies driving these changes, and future prospects for these industries.

10.1 AI in Financial Services

AI is profoundly impacting financial services, offering new ways to analyze data, manage risks, and deliver personalized customer experiences.

- **Fraud Detection and Prevention**: AI algorithms can analyze vast amounts of transaction data to detect unusual patterns and identify potential fraud. Machine learning models can adapt to new types of fraud, providing a dynamic and robust defense against fraudulent activities.

- **Risk Management**: AI helps financial institutions assess and manage risks more effectively. Predictive analytics models can analyze market trends, economic indicators, and financial data to forecast risks and make informed decisions. This greatly enhances the ability to mitigate risks and protect investments.

- **Credit Scoring**: Traditional credit scoring methods often rely on limited data. AI can analyze a broader range of data, including social media activity, payment histories, and online behaviors, to provide more accurate credit assessments. AI can help extend credit to underserved populations and improve financial inclusion.

- **Personalized Financial Services**: AI-powered chatbots and virtual assistants provide customers with personalized financial advice and support. These tools can answer queries, suggest financial products, and help customers manage their finances more effectively.

- **Algorithmic Trading**: AI-driven trading algorithms analyze real-time market data to execute trades at optimal times. These algorithms can quickly process vast amounts of information, identifying trading opportunities and minimizing risks. High-frequency trading firms rely heavily on AI to gain a competitive edge in the market.

10.2 AI in Business Operations

AI enhances business operations by automating processes, improving decision-making, and enabling data-driven insights.

- **Process Automation**: Robotic Process Automation (RPA) uses AI to automate repetitive and rule-based tasks, such as data entry, invoice processing, and customer support, increasing efficiency, reducing errors, and allowing employees to focus on more strategic activities.

- **Supply Chain Optimization**: AI analyzes data from various sources, including suppliers, logistics, and market trends, to optimize supply chain operations. Predictive analytics can forecast demand, identify potential disruptions, and recommend actions to ensure smooth and efficient supply chain management.

- **Customer Relationship Management (CRM)**: AI-enhanced CRM systems provide insights into customer behaviors, preferences, and needs. These systems can predict customer churn, recommend personalized marketing strategies, and improve customer engagement and retention.

- **Human Resources (HR)**: AI tools assist HR departments in recruiting, onboarding, and managing employees. AI-driven platforms can screen resumes, conduct initial interviews, and analyze employee performance data to identify high-potential candidates and areas for improvement.

- **Marketing and Sales**: AI algorithms analyze customer data to identify trends, segment audiences, and personalize marketing campaigns. Predictive analytics can forecast sales, optimize pricing strategies, and enhance the effectiveness of marketing efforts.

10.3 AI-Driven Decision Making

AI transforms decision-making processes by providing real-time insights, predictive analytics, and data-driven recommendations.

- **Business Intelligence (BI)**: AI-powered BI tools analyze large datasets to uncover hidden patterns, trends, and correlations. These tools provide actionable insights that help businesses make informed decisions, optimize operations, and identify new opportunities.

- **Predictive Analytics**: AI models predict future outcomes based on historical data, enabling businesses to anticipate market changes, customer behaviors, and operational challenges. Predictive analytics is used in various areas, including sales forecasting, inventory management, and financial planning.

- **Natural Language Processing (NLP)**: NLP technologies enable businesses to analyze and understand textual data, such as customer reviews, social media posts, and support tickets. Companies will gain insights into customer sentiment, identify emerging issues, and improve products and services.

10.4 AI in Financial Planning and Analysis

AI enhances financial planning and analysis (FP&A) by providing more accurate forecasts, automated reporting, and advanced analytics.

- **Financial Forecasting**: AI models analyze historical financial data and external factors to generate more accurate forecasts. These models can adapt to changing market conditions and provide real-time updates, helping businesses plan and allocate resources effectively.

- **Budgeting and Planning**: AI-driven tools streamline the budgeting process by automating data collection, consolidation, and analysis. These tools provide insights into spending patterns, identify cost-saving opportunities, and support strategic planning.

- **Performance Analysis**: AI analyzes financial performance data to identify trends, variances, and key performance indicators (KPIs). Businesses can then monitor their financial health, track progress toward goals, and make data-driven decisions.

10.5 Future Prospects of AI in Finance and Business

The future of AI in finance and business holds immense potential as technology continues to advance and new applications emerge.

- **AI-Powered Financial Advisors**: AI-driven financial advisors will provide more personalized and comprehensive financial planning services. These advisors will analyze a wide range of data, including financial goals, risk tolerance, and market trends, to offer tailored advice and investment strategies.

- **Autonomous Business Processes**: Integrating AI with other technologies like IoT and blockchain will enable fully autonomous business processes. For example, smart contracts on blockchain platforms can automate complex financial transactions, while IoT devices provide real-time data for decision-making.

- **Enhanced Customer Experiences**: AI will enable businesses to offer more personalized and seamless customer experiences. Advanced NLP and sentiment analysis will allow companies to understand and respond to customer needs more effectively, while AI-driven chatbots and virtual assistants will provide instant support and services.

- **Sustainable Finance**: AI can help financial institutions identify and invest in sustainable projects by analyzing environmental, social, and governance (ESG) data. This will support the transition to a more sustainable and responsible financial system.

10.6 Ethical and Regulatory Considerations

As AI becomes more integrated into finance and business, addressing ethical and regulatory considerations is crucial to ensure AI technologies' responsible and equitable use.

- **Data Privacy and Security**: Protecting customer data and ensuring privacy is paramount. Financial institutions and businesses must implement robust data protection measures and comply with privacy regulations to safeguard sensitive information.

- **Bias and Fairness**: AI models must be designed to avoid biases and ensure fairness. This involves using diverse datasets, continuously monitoring for biases, and implementing fairness constraints to prevent discriminatory outcomes.

- **Transparency and Accountability**: Ensuring transparency and accountability in AI-driven decision-making processes is essential. Businesses must clearly explain how AI models work, make decisions, and address potential issues.

- **Regulatory Compliance**: Financial institutions and businesses must comply with regulations governing AI and financial services. Compliance includes adhering to guidelines on data protection, algorithmic transparency, and ethical AI use.

10.7 Conclusion

AI is transforming the finance and business sectors by enhancing efficiency, improving decision-making, and providing innovative solutions to complex problems. AI is reshaping how organizations operate and compete, from fraud detection and risk management to personalized financial services and automated business processes. As AI technologies continue to advance, the future of finance and business holds exciting possibilities, but addressing ethical and regulatory considerations is essential to ensure responsible and equitable use of AI.

In the next chapter, we will explore the potential of quantum computing and its implications for AI, examining how this emerging technology could revolutionize AI capabilities and solve complex problems currently beyond the reach of classical computers.

CHAPTER 11

Quantum Computing and AI

Quantum computing is an emerging technology that promises to revolutionize AI by providing unprecedented computational power. This chapter explores the fundamentals of quantum computing, its potential applications in AI, and its transformative impact on solving complex problems currently intractable for classical computers. We will also discuss the challenges and future prospects of integrating quantum computing with AI.

11.1 Understanding Quantum Computing

Quantum computing leverages the principles of quantum mechanics to process information in fundamentally different ways than classical computing. While classical computers use bits as the basic unit of information, which can be either 0 or 1, quantum computers use quantum bits, or qubits, which can represent and process multiple states simultaneously due to the principles of superposition and entanglement.

- **Superposition**: A qubit can exist in a combination of 0 and 1 states simultaneously, allowing quantum computers to perform many calculations at once.

- **Entanglement**: Qubits can be entangled, meaning the state of one qubit is directly related to the state of another, no matter the distance between them. This property enables quantum computers to process complex correlations in data more efficiently than classical computers.

- **Quantum Gates**: Quantum gates manipulate qubits through operations analogous to classical logic gates, but they exploit quantum mechanical phenomena to perform complex calculations more quickly.

11.2 Potential Applications of Quantum Computing in AI

Quantum computing has the potential to significantly enhance AI by solving problems that are currently too complex for classical computers. Here are some key applications where quantum computing could make a significant impact:

- **Optimization Problems**: Many AI applications involve optimization problems, such as finding the best route for delivery trucks or optimizing supply chains. Quantum computing can explore multiple solutions simultaneously, finding optimal solutions much faster than classical methods.

- **Machine Learning**: Quantum machine learning algorithms can process and analyze large datasets more efficiently. Quantum algorithms, such as quantum support vector machines and quantum neural networks, can outperform their classical counterparts in classification, clustering, and regression tasks.

- **Drug Discovery**: Quantum computing can simulate molecular interactions at the quantum level, enabling more accurate modeling of complex biological systems. This can accelerate drug discovery by identifying promising compounds and more effectively predicting their behavior.

- **Cryptography**: Quantum computing poses both opportunities and challenges for cryptography. While it can break many classical cryptographic systems, it also enables the development of new quantum-resistant cryptographic techniques, ensuring secure communication in the quantum era.

- **Natural Language Processing (NLP)**: Quantum computing can enhance NLP by efficiently processing and analyzing large volumes of text data. Quantum algorithms can improve language translation, sentiment analysis, and text generation.

11.3 Quantum Machine Learning

Quantum machine learning is an interdisciplinary field that combines quantum computing and machine learning to develop new algorithms and techniques for solving complex problems.

- **Quantum Algorithms for Machine Learning**: Quantum versions of classical machine learning algorithms, such as quantum k-means clustering, quantum principal component analysis (PCA), and quantum reinforcement learning, leverage quantum parallelism to achieve speedups.

- **Variational Quantum Algorithms**: Variational algorithms use a combination of classical and quantum computations to optimize parameters for quantum circuits. These algorithms, such as the Variational Quantum Eigensolver (VQE) and Quantum Approximate Optimization Algorithm (QAOA), are used to solve optimization problems and machine learning tasks.

- **Quantum Data Encoding**: Efficiently encoding classical data into quantum states is a critical challenge. Techniques like amplitude encoding, binary encoding, and q-sampling are used to represent data in quantum systems.

11.4 Challenges and Limitations

Despite quantum computing's potential, several challenges and limitations must be addressed to realize its full potential in AI.

- **Quantum Hardware**: Building stable and scalable quantum hardware is a significant challenge. Quantum computers are highly sensitive to environmental noise, and maintaining qubit coherence and reducing error rates are critical for reliable computation.

- **Error Correction**: Quantum error correction is essential to protect quantum information from errors due to decoherence and other quantum noise. Developing efficient error-correcting codes and fault-tolerant quantum computing architectures is a major area of research.

- **Algorithm Development**: Designing efficient quantum algorithms that provide a clear advantage over classical algorithms is challenging. Researchers must identify problems where quantum speedups are achievable and develop practical algorithms to solve them.

- **Resource Requirements**: Quantum computers require significant resources, including cryogenic systems for cooling qubits and advanced control systems for qubit manipulation. Reducing the resource requirements and improving the scalability of quantum systems are essential for practical applications.

11.5 Future Prospects

The future of quantum computing and its integration with AI holds exciting possibilities as advancements in quantum hardware, algorithms, and applications continue to evolve.

- **Quantum Supremacy**: Achieving quantum supremacy, where quantum computers solve problems that are intractable for classical computers, is a key milestone. Researchers are working towards demonstrating quantum supremacy in practical applications, paving the way for broader adoption.

- **Hybrid Quantum-Classical Systems**: Hybrid systems that combine quantum and classical computing resources can leverage the strengths of both paradigms. These systems can perform complex quantum computations while relying on classical processors for certain tasks, enhancing overall performance and efficiency.

- **Industry Applications**: Quantum computing is expected to have a transformative impact on various industries, including finance, healthcare, logistics, and materials science. As quantum technology matures, more practical and commercially viable applications will emerge.

- **Collaboration and Research**: Continued collaboration between academia, industry, and government is essential for advancing quantum computing research. Investment in education, research, and infrastructure will drive innovation and accelerate the development of quantum technologies.

11.6 Conclusion

Quantum computing represents a paradigm shift in computational power, offering the potential to solve complex problems beyond the reach of classical computers. Its integration with AI promises to revolutionize fields such as optimization, machine learning, drug discovery, and cryptography. However, significant challenges remain, including developing stable quantum hardware, efficient error correction, and practical quantum algorithms. As research and development continue, the future of quantum computing and AI holds immense promise for transforming industries and advancing scientific discovery.

In the next chapter, we will explore the future of AI, examining emerging trends, potential societal impacts, and the ethical considerations that will shape the development and deployment of AI technologies in the years to come.

CHAPTER 12

The Future of AI: Trends, Impacts, and Ethical Considerations

As AI advances at an unprecedented pace, it is set to transform every aspect of society, from healthcare and education to finance and entertainment. The future of AI holds immense promise but also raises significant ethical, social, and economic challenges. In this chapter, we will explore the emerging trends in AI, the potential impacts on society, and the ethical considerations that will shape the development and deployment of AI technologies in the future.

12.1 Emerging Trends in AI

Several emerging trends are expected to drive the future of AI, leading to new capabilities and applications.

- **Explainable AI (XAI):** The need for transparency and interpretability grows as AI systems become more complex. Explainable AI aims to make AI models understandable to humans, enabling users to trust and effectively use AI decisions. Techniques like model-agnostic methods, visualization tools, and inherently interpretable models are advancing XAI.

- **Federated Learning**: Federated learning allows AI models to be trained across decentralized devices without sharing raw data, enhancing privacy and security. This approach is particularly beneficial for applications involving sensitive data, such as healthcare and finance, where data privacy is paramount.

- **AI for Good**: AI is increasingly being leveraged for social good, addressing global challenges such as climate change, healthcare, poverty, and education. AI-driven solutions are being developed to optimize energy usage, predict natural disasters, improve agricultural practices, and provide personalized education to underserved communities.

- **Human-AI Collaboration**: Future AI systems will focus on enhancing human capabilities rather than replacing them. Human-AI collaboration aims to create symbiotic relationships where AI augments human decision-making, creativity, and productivity. These relationships include developing intuitive and easy-to-use tools that seamlessly integrate AI into daily tasks.

- **Autonomous Systems**: The development of fully autonomous systems, such as self-driving cars, drones, and robots, will continue to advance. These systems will become more capable of operating independently in complex and dynamic environments, leading to new applications in transportation, logistics, and more.

- **Quantum AI**: The convergence of quantum computing and AI can potentially revolutionize the field. Quantum AI aims to leverage the computational power of quantum computers to solve complex problems currently infeasible for classical computers, such as large-scale optimization and advanced machine learning tasks.

12.2 Societal Impacts of AI

The widespread adoption of AI will profoundly impact society, affecting various aspects of daily life and the global economy.

- **Economic Transformation**: AI is expected to drive significant economic growth by improving productivity, creating new markets, and enabling innovative business models. However, this transformation will also lead to job displacement and changes in the labor market, necessitating reskilling and workforce development efforts.

- **Healthcare Advancements**: AI has the potential to revolutionize healthcare by enabling personalized medicine, improving diagnostics, and optimizing treatment plans. AI-driven tools can enhance patient care, reduce healthcare costs, and improve outcomes. However, ethical considerations around data privacy and equitable access must be addressed.

- **Education and Learning**: AI will transform education by providing personalized learning experiences, improving educational outcomes, and making education more accessible. AI-driven tools can support teachers, identify student needs, and facilitate lifelong learning. Ensuring equitable access to AI-powered education is essential to prevent widening educational disparities.

- **Social Interactions**: AI is reshaping social interactions through virtual assistants, chatbots, and social media algorithms. While these technologies can enhance connectivity and convenience, they also raise concerns about privacy, bias, and the impact on human relationships.

- **Environmental Sustainability**: AI can contribute to environmental sustainability by optimizing resource usage, reducing waste, and improving energy efficiency. AI-driven solutions can address environmental challenges, such as climate change, pollution, and biodiversity loss, by enabling better monitoring, prediction, and management.

12.3 Ethical Considerations in AI

As AI technologies become more pervasive, addressing ethical considerations is crucial to ensure their development and deployment align with societal values and human rights.

- **Bias and Fairness**: AI systems can inadvertently perpetuate and amplify biases present in training data, leading to unfair and discriminatory outcomes. Ensuring fairness in AI involves using diverse datasets, implementing bias detection and mitigation techniques, and continuously monitoring AI systems for biased behavior.

- **Data Privacy**: Using large datasets to train AI models raises significant privacy concerns. Protecting individuals' data and ensuring compliance with privacy regulations, such as GDPR and CCPA, is essential. Techniques like federated learning, differential privacy, and secure multi-party computation can enhance data privacy.

- **Transparency and Accountability**: AI systems should be transparent and accountable, enabling users to understand how decisions are made and who is responsible for them. Explainable AI, clear documentation, and robust governance frameworks are critical to ensuring accountability and building trust in AI technologies.

- **Autonomy and Control**: The deployment of autonomous systems raises questions about control and responsibility. Ensuring that humans remain in control and are able to override AI decisions when necessary is essential to prevent unintended consequences and maintain ethical standards.

- **Ethical AI Design**: It is crucial to incorporate ethical principles into the design and development of AI systems. This involves considering AI's societal impact, engaging with diverse stakeholders, and adhering to ethical guidelines and standards.

12.4 Preparing for an AI-Driven Future

Preparing for an AI-driven future requires proactive efforts from governments, organizations, and individuals to address the opportunities and challenges posed by AI.

- **Education and Workforce Development**: Investing in education and workforce development is essential to prepare individuals for the jobs of the future. This includes training in AI-related skills, promoting lifelong learning, and supporting reskilling and upskilling initiatives.

- **Policy and Regulation**: It is crucial to develop and implement policies and regulations that promote the ethical and responsible use of AI. Governments and regulatory bodies must work together to establish guidelines that ensure transparency, fairness, and accountability in AI deployment.

- **Research and Innovation**: Supporting research and innovation in AI is essential to drive technological advancements and address societal challenges. Collaborative efforts between academia, industry, and government can accelerate progress and ensure that AI benefits all of society.

- **Public Engagement**: Engaging the public in discussions about AI and its impact is crucial to building trust and ensuring that AI development aligns with societal values. Public awareness campaigns, forums, and consultations can facilitate informed debates and encourage responsible AI use.

12.5 Conclusion

The future of AI is filled with promise and potential, offering opportunities to enhance human capabilities, address global challenges, and improve quality of life. However, realizing this potential requires addressing ethical, social, and economic challenges to ensure that AI technologies are developed and deployed responsibly and equitably. By fostering collaboration, innovation, and ethical considerations, we can shape an AI-driven future that benefits all of humanity.

In the next chapter, we will conclude this book by summarizing the key insights and exploring the vision for the future of AI, highlighting the importance of responsible AI development and the need for continued efforts to harness AI's potential for the greater good.

CHAPTER 13

Conclusion: Shaping the Future of AI

As we conclude our exploration of AI and its profound impact on various aspects of our lives, it is clear that AI holds immense potential to transform industries, enhance human capabilities, and address some of the world's most pressing challenges. However, this transformative power also comes with significant responsibilities and ethical considerations. In this final chapter, we will summarize the key insights from our discussion and outline a vision for the future of AI, emphasizing the importance of responsible development and the collaborative efforts needed to harness AI's potential for the greater good.

13.1 Key Insights

Throughout this book, we have explored the multifaceted nature of AI, its applications, and its implications across various domains. Here are some of the key insights:

- **Advancements in AI**: The rapid advancements in machine learning, deep learning, and neural networks have enabled AI to achieve remarkable feats in areas such as natural language processing, computer vision, and autonomous systems. These technologies are the driving force behind the current AI revolution.

• **AI in Healthcare**: AI is revolutionizing healthcare by improving diagnostics, personalizing treatment plans, and enhancing patient care. AI-driven tools are transforming medical imaging, remote monitoring, and predictive analytics, leading to better health outcomes and reduced costs.

• **Autonomous Systems**: AI-powered autonomous systems, including self-driving cars, drones, and robots, are set to revolutionize transportation, logistics, and industrial automation. These systems offer significant benefits in terms of efficiency, safety, and sustainability.

• **Natural Language Processing (NLP)**: NLP enables machines to understand and interact with human language, transforming applications such as virtual assistants, translation services, and sentiment analysis. The ability to process and generate human language is a cornerstone of human-AI interaction.

• **Ethical and Responsible AI**: Addressing ethical considerations, such as bias, transparency, accountability, and privacy, is crucial for the responsible development and deployment of AI. Ensuring that AI technologies align with societal values and human rights is essential for building trust and ensuring equitable benefits.

- **AI in Education and Workforce Development**: AI is transforming education by providing personalized learning experiences, enhancing educational tools, and preparing individuals for future jobs. Lifelong learning and reskilling are essential to adapt to an AI-driven economy.

- **Integration with IoT and Edge Computing**: The convergence of AI with the Internet of Things (IoT) and edge computing is creating more intelligent, more responsive environments. This integration enables real-time data processing, improved decision-making, and enhanced efficiency across various industries.

- **AI in Creativity and Art**: AI is becoming an invaluable tool for artists and creators, enabling new forms of artistic expression and enhancing creative processes. AI-generated art, music, and literature challenge traditional notions of creativity and authorship.

- **AI in Finance and Business**: AI is revolutionizing finance and business by enhancing efficiency, improving decision-making, and providing innovative solutions to complex problems. Applications such as fraud detection, risk management, and personalized financial services are transforming these sectors.

- **Quantum Computing and AI**: Quantum computing can potentially revolutionize AI by providing unprecedented computational power. Integrating quantum computing and AI promises to solve complex problems currently intractable for classical computers.

13.2 A Vision for the Future of AI

The future of AI is filled with exciting possibilities, but realizing its full potential requires a shared vision that emphasizes responsible development, ethical considerations, and collaborative efforts. Here are some key elements of this vision:

- **Ethical AI Development**: Ensuring that AI technologies are developed and deployed ethically is paramount. This involves addressing issues of bias, transparency, accountability, and privacy. Ethical AI development requires the active participation of diverse stakeholders, including researchers, policymakers, industry leaders, and the public.

- **Human-Centric AI**: AI should be designed to enhance human capabilities and improve quality of life. Human-centric AI focuses on creating systems that support and augment human decision-making, creativity, and productivity. This approach prioritizes the needs and well-being of individuals and communities.

- **Equitable Access to AI**: Ensuring equitable access to AI technologies is essential to prevent widening disparities. Efforts should be made to bridge the digital divide, provide access to AI-powered education and healthcare, and promote inclusivity in AI development.

- **Collaborative Innovation**: Collaboration between academia, industry, government, and civil society is crucial for advancing AI research and development. Collaborative innovation can drive progress, address societal challenges, and ensure that AI benefits all of humanity.

- **Sustainable AI**: AI development should be guided by principles of sustainability. This includes minimizing the environmental impact of AI technologies, promoting energy-efficient computing, and leveraging AI to address environmental challenges such as climate change and resource management.

- **Continuous Learning and Adaptation**: The rapid pace of AI advancements requires constant learning and adaptation. Individuals, organizations, and societies must be prepared to adapt to changing technologies and evolving job markets. Lifelong learning and reskilling initiatives are essential for this adaptation.

13.3 The Role of Policymakers and Regulators

Policymakers and regulators play a critical role in shaping the future of AI. Their actions can promote ethical AI development, ensure equitable access, and protect public interests. Key areas for policymakers and regulators include:

- **Creating Regulatory Frameworks**: Developing clear and effective regulatory frameworks for AI is essential to address ethical and legal challenges. These frameworks should promote transparency, accountability, and fairness while encouraging innovation.

- **Supporting Research and Development**: Investing in AI research and development can drive technological advancements and address societal challenges. Governments should support initiatives that foster collaboration, innovation, and the responsible use of AI.

- **Promoting Public Awareness**: Engaging the public in discussions about AI and its implications is crucial for building trust and ensuring that AI development aligns with societal values. Public awareness campaigns, consultations, and educational programs can facilitate informed debates and decision-making.

- **Ensuring Data Privacy and Security**: Protecting individuals' data and ensuring compliance with privacy regulations is essential. Policymakers and regulators must establish robust data protection measures and promote practices that safeguard privacy and security.

13.4 Conclusion: A Call to Action

The future of AI is a collective endeavor that requires the active participation of all stakeholders. By embracing ethical principles, fostering collaboration, and promoting equitable access, we can shape an AI-driven future that benefits all of humanity. The journey ahead is filled with opportunities and challenges, but with a shared vision and concerted efforts, we can harness AI's transformative power for the greater good.

As we move forward, let us remain committed to the responsible development and deployment of AI, guided by the principles of fairness, transparency, accountability, and human-centricity. Together, we can create a future where AI enhances our lives, drives innovation, and addresses the global challenges of our time.

This concludes our exploration of the multifaceted world of AI. We hope this book has provided valuable insights into AI's current state and future prospects, inspiring you to engage with this transformative technology and contribute to shaping its future. Thank you for joining us on this journey, and we look forward to the exciting possibilities that lie ahead.

Appendices

Appendix A: Glossary of AI Terms

- **Artificial Intelligence (AI)**: The simulation of human intelligence processes by machines, particularly computer systems. These processes include learning, reasoning, and self-correction.

- **Machine Learning (ML)**: A subset of AI that involves the development of algorithms that allow computers to learn from and make predictions based on data.

- **Deep Learning**: A subset of machine learning involving neural networks with many layers that can model complex patterns in large amounts of data.

- **Neural Networks**: Computing systems inspired by the biological neural networks of animal brains. They consist of interconnected nodes (neurons) that process information.

- **Supervised Learning**: A type of machine learning where the model is trained on labeled data, learning to predict the output from the input data.

- **Unsupervised Learning**: A type of machine learning that deals with unlabeled data, aiming to identify hidden patterns or structures within the data.

- **Reinforcement Learning**: A type of machine learning where an agent learns to make decisions by taking actions in an environment to maximize some notion of cumulative reward.

- **Natural Language Processing (NLP)**: A field of AI that focuses on the interaction between computers and humans through natural language.

- **Computer Vision**: A field of AI that enables machines to interpret and make decisions based on visual data.

- **Generative Adversarial Networks (GANs)**: A class of machine learning frameworks where two neural networks compete against each other to generate new, synthetic instances of data.

- **Quantum Computing**: A type of computing that uses the principles of quantum mechanics to process information, leveraging qubits for greater computational power.

- **Edge Computing**: The practice of processing data near the edge of the network, where the data is generated, rather than in a centralized data-processing warehouse.

- **Internet of Things (IoT)**: A network of physical devices connected to the internet, capable of collecting and exchanging data.

Appendix B: Further Reading and Resources

Books:

1. *Artificial Intelligence: A Guide for Thinking Humans* by Melanie Mitchell

2. *Superintelligence: Paths, Dangers, Strategies* by Nick Bostrom

3. *Human Compatible: Artificial Intelligence and the Problem of Control* by Stuart Russell

4. *Life 3.0: Being Human in the Age of Artificial Intelligence* by Max Tegmark

5. *Prediction Machines: The Simple Economics of Artificial Intelligence* by Ajay Agrawal, Joshua Gans, and Avi Goldfarb

Journals and Magazines:

1. *Journal of Artificial Intelligence Research (JAIR)*

2. *IEEE Transactions on Neural Networks and Learning Systems*

3. *AI Magazine*

4. *Nature Machine Intelligence*

5. *Machine Learning Journal*

Websites and Online Courses:

1. Coursera: Machine Learning by Stanford University

2. edX: Artificial Intelligence by Columbia University

3. Khan Academy: Introduction to Artificial Intelligence

4. OpenAI: Research and Publications

5. MIT OpenCourseWare: Artificial Intelligence Courses

Conferences and Workshops:

1. NeurIPS (Neural Information Processing Systems)

2. ICML (International Conference on Machine Learning)

3. AAAI Conference on Artificial Intelligence

4. CVPR (Conference on Computer Vision and Pattern Recognition)

5. IJCAI (International Joint Conference on Artificial Intelligence)

Appendix C: Ethical AI Guidelines and Frameworks

Guidelines:

1. *Ethically Aligned Design* by IEEE

2. *AI Ethics Guidelines for Trustworthy AI* by the European Commission's High-Level Expert Group on AI

3. *The Montreal Declaration for Responsible AI*

4. *The Asilomar AI Principles* by the Future of Life Institute

5. *The Toronto Declaration: Protecting the Rights to Equality and Non-Discrimination in Machine Learning Systems*

Frameworks:

1. *Fairness, Accountability, and Transparency in Machine Learning (FAT/ML)*

2. *AI Now Institute's Framework for Algorithmic Impact Assessments*

3. *The Partnership on AI's Tenets for Ethical AI Development*

4. *AI4People's Ethical Framework for a Good AI Society*

5. *The OECD AI Principles*

Appendix D: AI Tools and Platforms

AI Development Platforms:

1. TensorFlow: An open-source platform for machine learning developed by Google.

2. PyTorch: An open-source machine learning library developed by Facebook's AI Research lab.

3. Keras: An open-source software library that provides a Python interface for artificial neural networks.

4. Scikit-learn: A machine learning library for Python.

5. Microsoft Azure Machine Learning: A cloud-based environment for training, deploying, and managing machine learning models.

AI Tools:

1. OpenAI GPT-3: A state-of-the-art language model capable of generating human-like text.

2. IBM Watson: A suite of AI tools and applications designed for business.

3. Google Cloud AI: A collection of machine learning tools and services.

4. Amazon SageMaker: A fully managed service that provides every developer and data scientist with the ability to build, train, and deploy machine learning models quickly.

5. RapidMiner: A data science platform for machine learning and predictive analytics.

Bibliography

Books:

1. Agrawal, A., Gans, J., & Goldfarb, A. (2018). *Prediction Machines: The Simple Economics of Artificial Intelligence.* Harvard Business Review Press.

2. Bostrom, N. (2014). *Superintelligence: Paths, Dangers, Strategies.* Oxford University Press.

3. Mitchell, M. (2019). *Artificial Intelligence: A Guide for Thinking Humans.* Farrar, Straus and Giroux.

4. Russell, S. (2019). *Human Compatible: Artificial Intelligence and the Problem of Control.* Viking.

5. Tegmark, M. (2017). *Life 3.0: Being Human in the Age of Artificial Intelligence.* Knopf.

Journal Articles:

1. Goodfellow, I., Pouget-Abadie, J., Mirza, M., Xu, B., Warde-Farley, D., Ozair, S., ... & Bengio, Y. (2014).

Generative adversarial nets. *Advances in Neural Information Processing Systems, 27,* 2672-2680.

2. LeCun, Y., Bengio, Y., & Hinton, G. (2015). Deep learning. *Nature, 521*(7553), 436-444.

3. Silver, D., Huang, A., Maddison, C. J., Guez, A., Sifre, L., Van Den Driessche, G., ... & Hassabis, D. (2016). Mastering the game of Go with deep neural networks and tree search. *Nature, 529*(7587), 484-489.

Conferences:

1. Bengio, Y., Ducharme, R., Vincent, P., & Jauvin, C. (2003). A neural probabilistic language model. In *Journal of Machine Learning Research* (pp. 1137-1155).

2. Devlin, J., Chang, M. W., Lee, K., & Toutanova, K. (2019). BERT: Pre-training of Deep Bidirectional Transformers for Language Understanding. In *Proceedings of the 2019 Conference of the North American Chapter of the Association for Computational Linguistics: Human Language Technologies* (pp. 4171-4186).

Websites and Online Resources:

1. OpenAI. (2023). GPT-3. Retrieved from https://www.openai.com/research/gpt-3.

2. IBM. (2023). IBM Watson. Retrieved from https://www.ibm.com/watson.

3. Google AI. (2023). Google Cloud AI. Retrieved from https://cloud.google.com/products/ai.

4. Amazon Web Services. (2023). Amazon SageMaker. Retrieved from https://aws.amazon.com/sagemaker.

Reports and Guidelines:

1. European Commission. (2020). AI Ethics Guidelines for Trustworthy AI. Retrieved from https://ec.europa.eu/futurium/en/ai-alliance-consultation/guidelines.

2. IEEE. (2021). Ethically Aligned Design: A Vision for Prioritizing Human Well-being with Autonomous and Intelligent Systems. IEEE Standards Association. Retrieved from https://standards.ieee.org/industry-connections/ec/autonomous-systems.html.

Educational Resources:

1. Ng, A. (2023). Machine Learning. Coursera. Retrieved from https://www.coursera.org/learn/machine-learning.

2. Columbia University. (2023). Artificial Intelligence. edX. Retrieved from https://www.edx.org/course/cs50s-introduction-to-artificial-intelligence-with-python.

Acknowledgments and Contributions:

1. Future of Life Institute. (2017). The Asilomar AI Principles. Retrieved from https://futureoflife.org/ai-principles/.

2. Partnership on AI. (2023). Tenets for Ethical AI Development. Retrieved from https://www.partnershiponai.org/tenets/.

This bibliography provides a comprehensive list of resources and references that informed the content of this book. We hope that these materials will serve as valuable resources for readers who wish to further explore the fascinating world of AI. Thank you for your interest and engagement in the future of artificial intelligence.

Made in the USA
Columbia, SC
04 September 2024

41656461R00065